HAL•LEONARD
Classical
PLAY-ALONG™

Volume 12

Michel
de la BARRE
(ca. 1674-1744)

Soprano (Descant) Recorder Suite No. 9 "Deuxième Livre" in G Major

ISBN 978-1-4234-6251-4

HAL•LEONARD®
CORPORATION

7777 W. BLUEMOUND RD. P.O. BOX 13819 MILWAUKEE, WI 53213

In Australia Contact:
Hal Leonard Australia Pty. Ltd.
4 Lentara Court
Cheltenham, Victoria, 3192 Australia
Email: ausadmin@halleonard.com.au

Visit Hal Leonard Online at
www.halleonard.com

Preface

The Hal Leonard Classical Play-Along™ series allows you to work through great classical works systematically and at any tempo with accompaniment.

Tracks 2-4 on the CD demonstrate the concert version of each movement. After tuning your instrument to Track 1 you can begin practicing the piece. Using the Amazing Slow-Downer technology included on the CD, you can adjust the recording to any tempo you like without altering the pitch. (Note that when using Amazing Slow-Downer, the CD will stop after each track instead of playing continuously.)

- Track No. ☐1☐ – tuning notes
- Track numbers in circles ◯ – concert version
- Track numbers in diamonds ◆ – play-along version

CONCERT VERSION

Manfredo Zimmerman, Soprano (Descant) Recorder

Mechthild Winter, Harpsichord

Steffen Hoffmann, Cello

SUITE NO. 9

for Soprano (Descant) Recorder in G Major

"Deuxieme Livre"

I ②

M. de la Barre (ca. 1674 - ca. 1744)

Sonate l'Inconnue

II ③

7 Vivement

8

9

10

(Gravement)

III ④

11 Chaconne

61

67

71

77

13

85

92

100

107

112

116